ERA	PERIOD		MEANING	Millions of Years		EVENTS
				Duration	Ago	
AZOIC	PRE-CAMBRIAN		Means before the Cambrian.	about 2600	4600	Earth forms
						First rocks
					about 2000	Life begins
ROTEROZOIC				about 1430		First forms of life
PALAEOZOIC or PRIMARY	CAMBRIAN		Named after Cambria, an ancient name for Wales.	70	570	
	ORDOVICIAN		Named after a tribe of ancient Britons, the Ordovices.	60	500	Age of sea creatures
						Earliest fishes
	SILURIAN		Named after a tribe, the Silures.	45	440	
	DEVONIAN		Named after Devon.	50	395	Age of fishes
	CARBONIFEROUS		Means coal bearing.	65	345	Earliest amphibians
					280	Age of amphibians Earliest reptiles
	PERMIAN		Named after Perm in the Ural Mountains.	55		
MESOZOIC or SECONDARY	TRIASSIC		Means 3 divisions.	30	225	Earliest mammals
	JURASSIC		Named after the Jura Mountains.	59	195	Earliest birds Age of reptiles
	CRETACEOUS		Named after creta, the Latin word for chalk.	71	136	Reptile extinction
CENOZOIC	Tertiary	PALAEOCENE		9	65	
		EOCENE		16	54	
		OLIGOCENE	All names refer to shells similar to types alive in our seas today.	12	38	Age of mammals
		MIOCENE		19	26	
		PLIOCENE		5	7	
	Quaternary	PLEISTOCENE	Means most recent.	1	2	Ice ages Age of man

About 4,500 million years ago the Earth came into being.
Time passed – millions and millions of years – as the Earth cooled.
Then, about 600 million years ago, life began to develop.

The first minute living things – tiny plants,
bacteria and viruses – appeared in the seas,
releasing life-giving oxygen.
Gradually the seas became filled with living creatures.
After another few million years came the fish,
followed by the amphibians and then the reptiles.

We know a great deal about those strange-looking early animals
and the world they lived in, from fossils found
in the Earth's rock layers.
We know what they ate, what they looked like,
and how they lived and died.

Fascinating evidence of early life can be found by anyone,
and this beautifully illustrated book
will show you what to look for and how to identify
what you find.

Dinosaurs and Prehistoric Animals

by GRAHAM WELLFARE B Sc

with illustrations by
BERNARD ROBINSON *and* ROBERT AYTON

MODERN PUBLISHING
A Division of Unisystems, Inc.
New York, New York 10022
Printed in Belgium

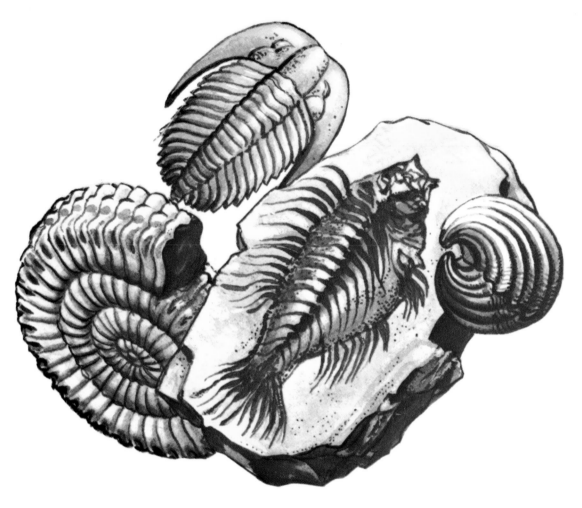

Stories in the stones

How do we know so much about animals that roamed the Earth millions of years ago?

Most of what we have learned comes from *fossils*. A fossil is usually the remains of an animal or plant that has been preserved. Sometimes it is just the impression of where an animal has once been. By using the word *animal*, we mean all land and sea creatures from the smallest shrimp to the biggest dinosaur. Often fossils are found in rock, but occasionally they are found in other substances.

A fossil may be a shell, a bone, a tooth, a horn or a claw. It may be a whole animal. It may be only its footprint. Yet even a footprint can tell us how an animal walked or ran. Each fossil that is found adds to our knowledge of animals that lived long, long ago. So it is important that we know where fossils come from.

Skeleton on lake shore

Lake rises and covers skeleton

In time, sediment covers skeleton completely

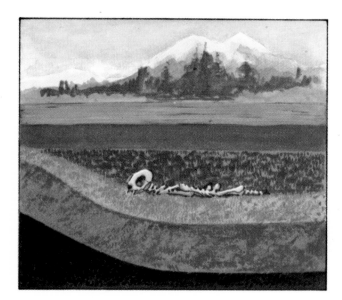

Under pressure, sediment becomes solid rock

Millions of years later the rock is exposed and eroded, and the fossil skeleton revealed

How did the fossil get in the rock?

A rock as you know is extremely hard. (We often say 'as solid as a rock.') Yet fossils are often found right in the middle of the most solid rock. The story of how they got there begins in the distant past.

Imagine yourself standing on the shore of a lake, millions and millions of years ago. A sabre-toothed tiger has just died, and with many hungry animals about, the skin and flesh do not last long. Soon there is only a skeleton, lying on the lake shore. The depth of the lake, like rivers and lakes of today, will vary according to how much rain there has been. When it has rained heavily, the waters of the lake will rise and cover the skeleton. In time the position or depth of the lake may change so that the bones are permanently covered by water. It is the time that the skeleton spends under the water that is so important.

Today, and for millions of years past, small, light grains of dust and dirt have been swept from the land in rainstorms and in permanent streams and brooks. They are carried into big, slow-flowing rivers, into lakes, and into the sea. Here they slowly sink to the bottom as particles of what is called *sediment*.

So if we return to our lake of many years ago, we find the bones being slowly buried in sediment. Soon the remains are quite invisible, sunk below the lake bed. As the bones become deeper and deeper, the sediment above them gets heavier and heavier. The particles of sediment are crushed together, and the water is squeezed out. At length, the weight above is so great that the sediment becomes quite solid. It has become rock. Somewhere in that rock lies the skeleton of the sabre-toothed tiger. After all this time it may certainly be called a fossil.

Millions of years pass. Sabre-toothed tigers have now become *extinct* (there are none left). The lake has dried up, and slowly the wind and rain begin to wear away the rock covering the fossil bones. Eventually the bone closest to the surface begins to show through. Now it might be discovered and collected. If not, it too will begin to wear away.

Where can you find fossils? Why are they so rare?

Rocks containing fossils exist in almost every part of the world, but most of them are hidden under the ground. You probably walk or ride over some every day. The fossils may be just below the surface or many hundreds of feet below. We do not know exactly where or how deep such fossils occur. This uncertainty makes underground fossils very hard to find. However, fossils can be collected where rocks containing fossils come to the surface. This happens most often at seaside cliffs, or where a river or stream cuts deeply into the ground.

Fossils are also discovered where men mine or quarry. At coal mines, chalk quarries, stone quarries, gravel pits and clay pits, fossils are often thrown aside while the more valuable minerals are removed. Some fossils are so close to the surface that they are ploughed out of fields. You may even be lucky enough to find a fossil while digging in your garden.

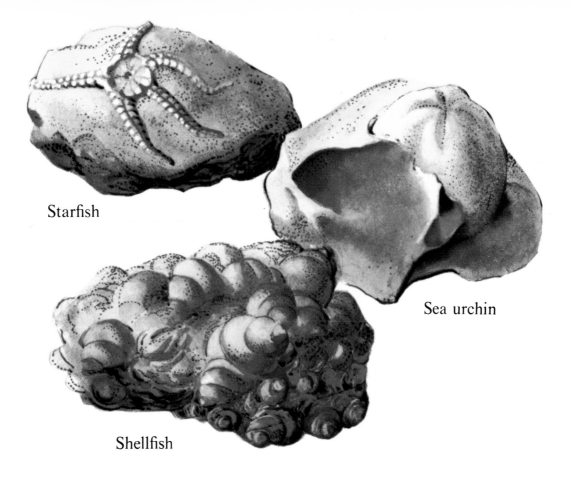

Starfish

Sea urchin

Shellfish

Not all fossils found are bones. Many rocks contain more fossils of shells, sea urchins, starfish and other small creatures than they do of bones. Sometimes, what looks like a band of rock may itself be a vast fossil. It is a prehistoric coral reef. Such a reef might be miles long and many feet high! On the other hand, some fossils are so small that they can be seen only through a microscope. Prehistoric pollen grains often have to be looked at in this way.

A living ammonite settling on the sea bed 180 million years ago

Other ways in which fossils are formed

Sometimes the fossil itself dissolves away. It may be replaced by some other substance, such as silica or golden iron pyrites (often called 'fool's gold') or calcite (a form of limestone). When this happens, the new substance takes up the exact shape of the object which has disappeared.

The reason that this happens is quite simple. When the sediment is being crushed into rock, it presses closely against the fossil. After the rock is formed, the original fossil begins to dissolve away. This leaves a hole in the rock the exact shape and size of the object that has disappeared.

Because they are always exposed to the damp, rocks usually have small amounts of water seeping through them.

This water deposits very small amounts of certain minerals, such as calcite, in the space. Slowly, over millions of years, the hole fills up with the calcite.

Since the hole was exactly the same shape and size as the original fossil, the new calcite fossil is also of that shape and size. When such fossils are broken open, the calcite fossil can sometimes be taken out of the surrounding rock.

The calcite fossil is called the *cast*. The hole left behind in the rock, which bears the shape of the fossil, is called the *mold*. So you could almost say that you are getting two fossils for the price of one!

The mold can also be used as a model mold, if it is not too damaged. First, it must be varnished for protection. Then latex rubber or warm wax or some other modeling substance is poured into the two halves of the mold. This should produce a copy of the fossil.

An ammonite fossil found today

There are other, rarer, types of fossils. When prehistoric animals came to the banks of rivers and lakes to drink, they often left tracks in the soft mud at the edge of the water. If it was a dry summer, then the lake or river might have become shallower, and not have covered the footprints again until autumn. The mud would then have baked hard in the hot summer sun. When autumn came, the mud containing the track might have been baked so hard that the water did not soften it again. Sediment would have fallen into the footprints, making a separate new layer. Then the sediment and mud would have turned to stone as described earlier.

When a rock is formed by sediment falling on already hardened mud, the rock often splits between the sediment layer and the baked mud layer. This makes prehistoric animal tracks quite easy to uncover, once they have been found.

A dinosaur footprint left in mud,
baked hard and preserved for millions of years

Many fossil bones are coated with plaster of Paris before being removed from the site. This protects the bones and keeps any broken pieces in place during transport

Next, the bones must be taken out of the rock. How this is done depends on the type of rock. If the rock is soft, the bones can be dug out (carefully of course to avoid damage). If they are in a thin layer of rock, the whole layer can be taken up and carried back to the museum. The bones can then be extracted later. If the rock is hard and thick, a slow careful process of removal by chipping around each individual bone takes place.

Sometimes the bone looks very fragile, or may have become weakened while it was being removed from the rock. If this is the case, the bone is treated while it lies in the rock. Sometimes, it is only necessary to strengthen the bone with a liquid plastic substance. This seeps through all the fossil, then hardens, giving it extra strength.

Fractured and broken bones are treated just like a hospital treats broken limbs – they are given a plaster cast. In any case, larger bones are generally transported coated in plaster, to protect them. Smaller bones are usually cushioned in foam or some other soft substance. After weeks, or perhaps months, all the bones exposed at last reach the museum – but there is still a good deal to do!

13

When they arrive at the museum, the bones are unpacked and taken out of the plaster. The first job is to clean any unwanted rock from the fossil. Sometimes the bones are completely freed of rock. On other occasions, the skeleton may be fairly flat, and the bones arranged in a lifelike manner. Then it is best to leave the fossil in the slab of rock for protection. The rock is simply cleaned back a little, to show the bones up better.

Cleaning is done in one of several ways. Ultrasonic baths vibrate the fossil so that any loose grains of rock are shaken off. There is a machine which blows hard dust at the rock and wears it away.

Fossils can also be cleaned by dissolving away the unwanted rock in certain acids. All these methods have to be used very carefully, to avoid damage to the fossil. After being cleaned up, each bone must be repaired and protected. Broken bones are stuck back together, using a special glue. Holes can be filled in with plaster of Paris.

Finally, a protective coat of plastic varnish is put over the whole bone, to help to prevent further decay and damage. The bones which have been prepared separately must now be put together to form a skeleton.

Here the grid map prepared earlier begins to help. The people assembling the skeleton know that the bones that go together in the skeleton are usually found close together on the grid. Nevertheless, it is not an easy job to put a skeleton together, and it is not always done correctly. When the Iguanodon was first discovered, for example, it was assembled as a four-legged animal with a horn on its nose. Later, people discovered that the Iguanodon stood on two legs, and that its 'horn' was really a thumb bone!

It is very seldom that a complete skeleton is found. If not, the people working on the fossil look at other fossils of the same animal, if there are any. This will tell them the shape of the missing bones. Now they will make them up, in plaster of Paris, to the right size for their animal. Once all the fossil and plaster of Paris bones for a complete skeleton have been obtained, they can be put together. With no muscle holding the bones together, each bone must be separately supported.

The skeletons of big dinosaurs such as Brontosaurus need many heavy metal bars and strong metal cables to support them. Eventually, the skeleton stands complete, and is put on display in the museum.

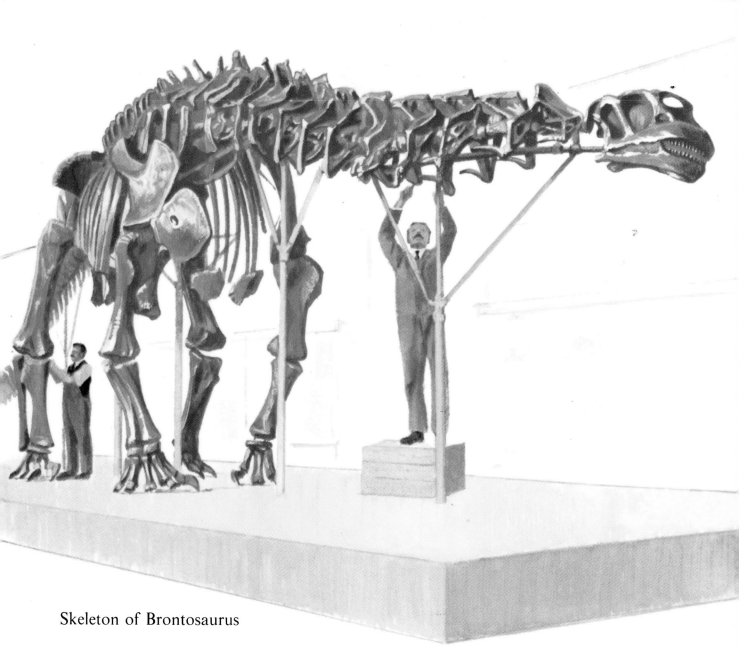

Skeleton of Brontosaurus

What a lot of work there has been between finding the first bone, and putting the skeleton on show! It is then the turn of the museum's artists to study the skeleton. They will make an accurate drawing of how the prehistoric animal probably looked, when it was alive and roaming the Earth!

How life began

Scientists believe that the Earth was formed four and a half thousand million years ago. For millions of years, it must have been so hot that all the ground was molten. The heat of the molten rock boiled all the water into scalding steam. The steam formed great clouds, which blotted out the sun. There was no oxygen in the air. Instead, the atmosphere was made up of poisonous gases and steam. On that hot gloomy poisonous world, nothing breathed, nothing lived.

Over hundreds of millions of years, the planet gradually cooled down. First the ground became solid. It was still too hot for the steam to become water. So there were no rivers, lakes or seas.

The molten core of the Earth was closer to the surface than today. There were volcanoes and lakes of boiling lava everywhere. Later, the Earth had cooled enough for the steam to turn to water. The steam clouds turned to thunder clouds.

It rained, without stopping, for millions of years. It rained until the oceans and seas had formed. While it rained, the only light under the heavy thunderclouds came from flashes of lightning, and the fire and glowing lava from volcanoes. There was still no sign of life in the sea, or on the land. Before long, the rain slowly eased off. The clouds thinned, and the sun burst through. Above the clouds, most of the poisonous gases had gradually been lost into space. Now the atmosphere was almost free of them.

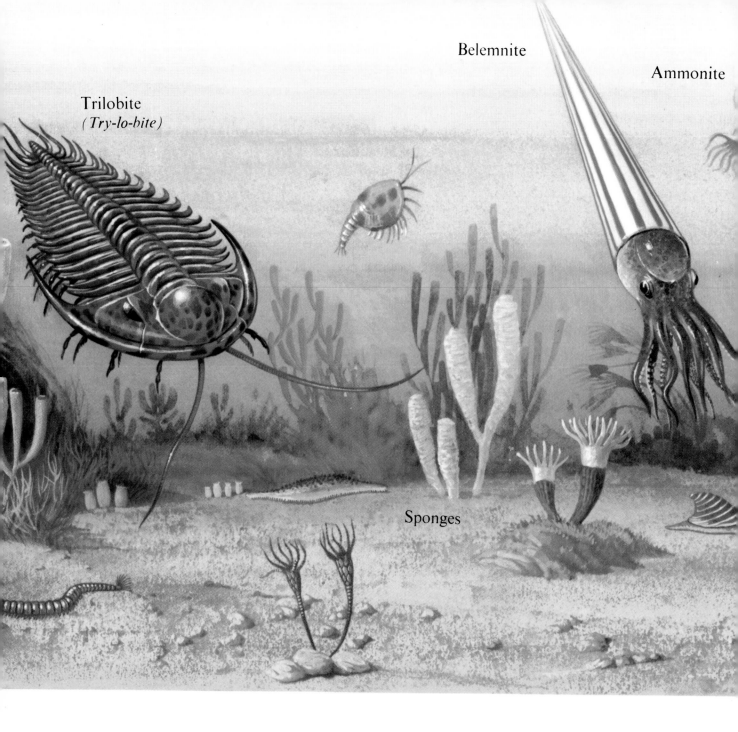

Belemnite

Ammonite

Trilobite
(*Try-lo-bite*)

Sponges

In the seas, the first living things appeared. They were very small, like *bacteria* and *viruses* (germs). There were also *algae* (tiny plants) in those early seas. Millions upon millions of them released life-giving oxygen.

The outer layers of the atmosphere formed, and prevented the oxygen from escaping into space. A few million years later, the earliest sea creatures appeared. At first they were only small and simple forms of life. Then gradually larger and more complicated ones also began to appear.

So by five hundred million years ago, the sea was filled with living creatures. Corals, anemones, sponges and the beautiful *crinoids* (sea-lilies) grew from the sea bed. Bivalves, such as the oyster and mussel, along with brachiopods, which looked like bivalves, sat on the sand. Worms, sea snails, starfish and sea urchins crawled over the bottom. Jellyfish floated in the sea. *Ammonites* and *belemnites* (early relatives of the squid) and primitive shrimp-like creatures swam in the water. Most common of all were the peculiar *trilobites*. However, there were not yet any fish.

The first fish appeared in the oceans about four hundred and fifty million years ago. They looked quite strange compared with the fish that we know today. None of them had moving jaws, but their mouths were always open. In front of the mouth there was a row of filters to strain food through from the sea. Many had a shield of bony armor completely surrounding their heads. Most of them had spines or flat bony plates, instead of movable fins. They were seldom large: *Pteraspis* was about 6 inches long.

The earliest fish with biting jaws had movable fins. This gave them added stability in the water. However, they still had bony armor around the head. These fish could grow to a much larger size. *Dinichthys*, at 30.2 feet long, was as long as a bus!

Dinichthys
(*Din-ik-this*)

Pteraspis
(*Tair-as-pis*)

These first fish were replaced in the oceans by fish with no bony armor. Instead, some had bony skeletons and scales all over their bodies. Others, the early sharks and rays, had skeletons made not of bone but of a softer substance called *cartilage*. Even today, sharks and rays differ from other fish in this way. In the shallow, swampy seas of four hundred to three hundred million years ago, many different groups of fish grew in numbers, then dwindled or disappeared.

Three main groups of fish evolved: the ray-finned fish, the lung-fish and the lobe-finned fish. The ray-finned fish all had bony spines supporting their fins. They went on to form almost all the modern groups of fish.

Life moves onto the land

Around four hundred million years ago, the land began to rise as a great period of mountain building began. Some types of seaweed were left behind as the water level fell. This meant that they had to try to survive on land. They developed roots, to absorb moisture, stems for support, and leathery skins to their leaves, to prevent them from drying up.

At first the plants were small, and stayed close to the water's edge, because they needed the moisture. Later, taller plants with deeper roots appeared. They did not need to stay so close to the sea or lake shores.

All the plants were relatives of today's mosses and ferns: what we call *soft vegetation* because they have pulpy rather than woody stems. However, some of the soft vegetation of those days was very strange. Imagine a moss as tall as a tree! These and other plants died, fell and were buried. Then they slowly fossilized, to form the coal and oil deposits that are so precious to us today. Sometimes you can see the pattern of a leaf or branch on a lump of coal.

For millions of years, these plants grew all over the Earth, but there were no animals or insects living on the land at all. Living creatures could be found only underwater. Then the first creatures, primitive insects, left the water for a life on land.

After some time, scorpions, spiders and millipedes lived along the lake shores. Then the first land snails came ashore. Later dragonflies as big as birds, with a 24 inch wingspan, and huge 4 inch cockroaches, flew in amongst the ferns.

Tree ferns and other early plant life

Lobe-fin fish

About three hundred and fifty million years ago, a long age of seasonal droughts began. Every year, some of the lakes and swamps would begin to dry up. They might leave a few small, stagnant pools and puddles. They might completely dry out! The animals living in these lakes and swamps had to find a way to survive the dry season.

A fish breathes by using its gills to absorb oxygen dissolved in water. The oxygen in small pools is quickly used up. So lung-fish developed lungs, to enable them to gulp mouthfuls of air when there is no oxygen left in the water.

Another group of fish, the lobe-fins mentioned earlier (*Eusthenopteron* for instance), went still further. They had two front fins and two back fins, all heavy and muscular, and a stronger backbone.

If their pool dried out completely, they were able to drag themselves to a new one, using their strong fins. On the way, they could breathe air. The lobe-fins grew up to 24 inches long, about the size of a salmon.

After millions of years, the fins of the lobe-finned fish had developed into the short legs of the amphibian. The word *amphibian* means an animal able to live both on land and in water.

One of the first amphibians was called *Ichthyostega*. Its feet were webbed, and its tail had a fin on it. Ichthyostega probably spent most of its time in the water, because it was not well protected against drying out when it was on land. The first amphibians probably fed on land. They ate insects and snails. However, they had to return to the water to lay their eggs. Ichthyostega was probably about 36 inches long.

Ichthyostega
(Ik-thee-oh-steega)

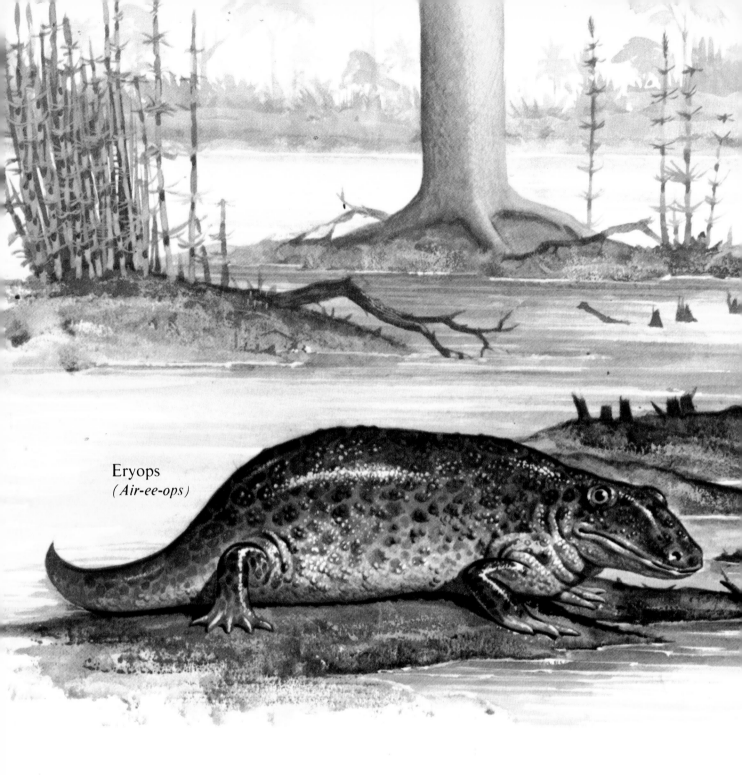

Eryops
(*Air-ee-ops*)

By three hundred million years ago, the swamps were filled with many different sorts of amphibians. Some were only 2 inches long. Others, such as *Eogyrinus*, grew as long as 14.8 feet. Some now ate smaller amphibians instead of insects.

Amphibians no longer had any fins on their tails, and their feet were less webbed than before. Their skins were tougher, so they probably spent much more time out of the water. However, they still stayed among the swamps and pools, and still had to lay their eggs in water.

Eogyrinus
(Ee-oh-jy-rine-us)

Modern amphibians such as the frog, toad and newt are thought to have come from creatures like *Eryops.* Eryops was a medium-sized amphibian, measuring 5 feet in length, about the same as the common seal.

For many millions of years, amphibians ruled the Earth. Then about two hundred and twenty five million years ago, more mountain building began. The climate became dryer, and many lowland swamps were lost. A new type of animal, better suited to live in these conditions, began to take over. This was the reptile.

Reptiles inherit the Earth

This new type of animal was a descendant of the amphibians. Reptiles did not need to enter the water at any time. They still returned to water to drink, and sometimes to bathe. However, their eggs now had leathery shells to prevent them from drying out. So unlike the amphibians, reptiles laid their eggs on dry land. *Seymouria* was one of the first reptiles. It was 24 inches long, and still looked quite like an amphibian. Probably it ate the same sort of food as the amphibians.

As reptiles became larger and more numerous, more varied types, which looked less like amphibians, began to appear. *Edaphosaurus* was a fin-back or sail-back reptile. Reptiles do not control the temperature of their bodies like we do. It is thought that the 'sail' of the fin-back reptile was used to catch the sun and warm the reptile up, and to help it to lose heat into the air when it was too hot. Edaphosaurus was about 9 feet long, and was one of the first animals to learn how to eat land plants.

Seymouria
(*See-more-ee-ya*)

Dimetrodon was another fin-back reptile, probably the best known among them. It was 9 feet long, but was not as heavy as the plant-eating Edaphosaurus. Dimetrodon was a much more agile animal. This was very important, for it was a meat eater. It lived on smaller amphibians and reptiles, and probably had to run in order to catch them. At the highest point, its sail could be 7 feet high, taller than a man! The fin-backs were members of a group of reptiles called the *synapsids*.

Later synapsids had no sails. *Dicynodon*, one of the most successful synapsids, had a peculiarly shaped head. It was broad and flat, and the females were usually entirely without teeth. The males had huge tusks curving from their upper jaws, but no other teeth. Instead of teeth, the jaws were covered by a horny beak. Dicynodon was a heavily built animal, with short, stubby legs. Its size ranged from 2 inches up to 14.8 feet.

Edaphosaurus
(*Ee-daf-oh-sawrus*)

Dimetrodon
(*Di-meet-ro-don*)

Strangely enough, after having conquered the land, some reptiles returned to the seas. Some spent all their time in water, while others were able to come out onto land to lay their eggs, as turtles do today. Among the first reptiles to return to the sea were the *nothosaurs*, such as *Ceresiosaurus*. These were medium-sized animals, about 3 feet in length, quite heavily built, with a long neck, a fairly large head, and a long tail. Their limbs were rather long for swimming, but their feet were paddle-like and probably webbed. They could come out onto the seashore and probably ate fish.

The *placodonts*, such as *Placodus*, were another group that returned to the sea after a few million years on land. They ate only bivalves and other shelled animals from the sea bed. Placodonts were seal-shaped, about 4 feet long, and some had bony plates, like a turtle shell, on their backs. They swam about in shallow water, scooping up shells and crushing them with their huge flattened teeth.

Later, many water-dwelling reptiles never returned to dry land, even to lay eggs. The eggs hatched inside the females, and the young were born live. *Ichthyosaurus* was a very fish-like reptile. Its limbs had turned into fins and its tail was a flattened paddle, like a fish tail. This reptile had a long beak, with many sharp teeth for catching fish. It probably looked like a dolphin, except that some were much larger, up to 30 feet in length.

Ichthyosaurus
(*Ik-thee-oh-sawrus*)

The *plesiosaurs*, such as *Plesiosaurus*, also lived permanently in the sea. They were a quite different shape from the Ichthyosaurs. Their bodies were broad and flat, and they swam by a sort of rowing movement with their four powerful flippers. They had long slender necks which helped them to catch fish. Unlike the earlier nothosaurs, their heads were small and their tails were short. Plesiosaurs were often large, and could be more than 40 feet long, almost as long as a railroad car. The Loch Ness Monster legend is thought to be based on the survival of a plesiosaur.

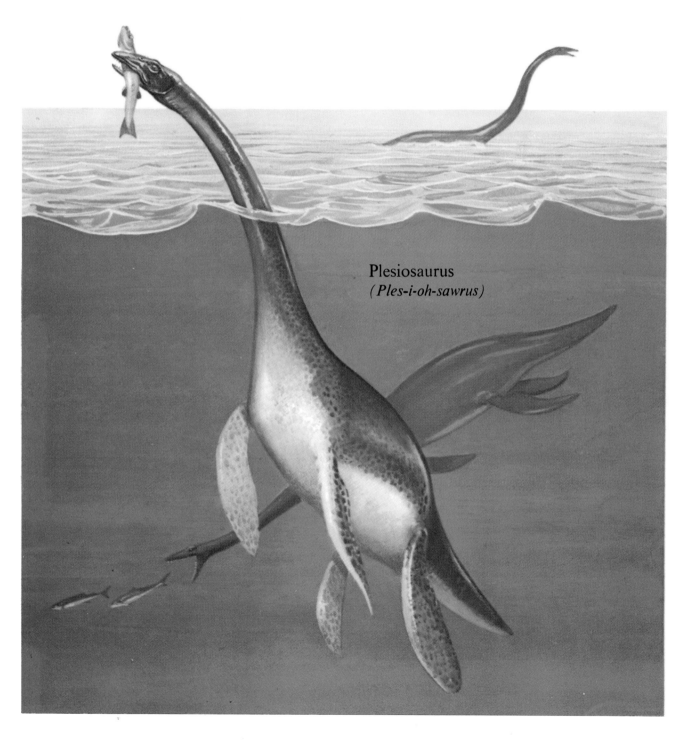

Plesiosaurus
(*Ples-i-oh-sawrus*)

More than one group of reptiles took to the air. One group
developed feathers and became the birds of today. We will talk
about them later. The other group were the *pterosaurs*. These were
not true flying reptiles. They glided, using the winds and air
currents to keep them aloft. In this way, they resembled bats, rather
than birds. Their wings were made out of a thin layer of skin,
stretched out along an enormously long fourth finger on each hand,
then across to meet the leg, usually joining it between the knee and
the ankle. The bones of the pterosaurs were often small and hollow
so that they did not weigh the creatures down.

Pterodactylus
(*Tair-oh-dak-till-us*)

It is thought that these gliding reptiles lived on sea cliffs, and ate fish. The breezes off the sea would have helped them to glide. There were two types of pterosaurs. Both the hawk-sized *Rhamphor-hynchus*, with a wing span of 36.4 inches, and the almost eagle-sized *Dimorphodon*, whose wing span was 3.9 feet, had long tails and many teeth. The smaller *Pterodactylus*, however, with a 12 inch wing span, had fewer teeth and no tail.

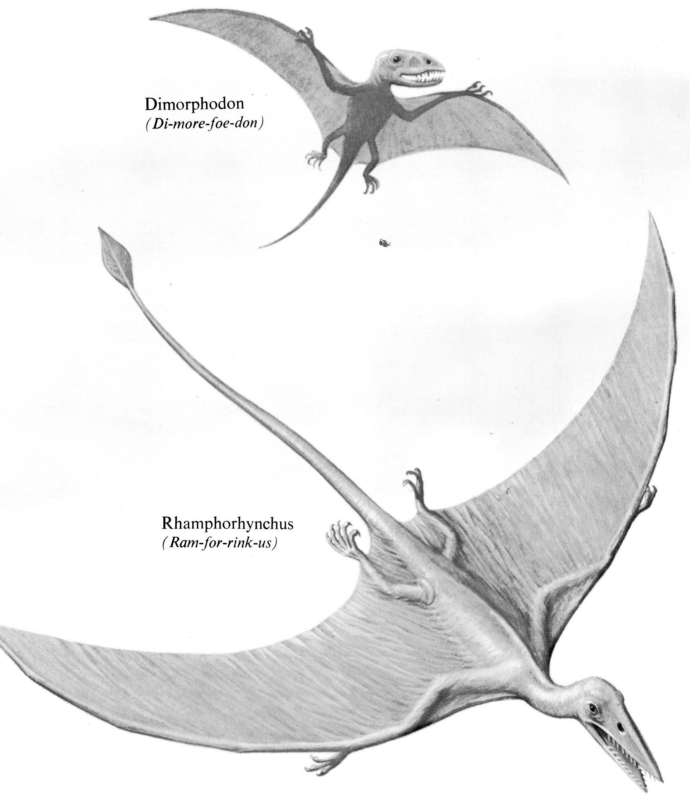

Dimorphodon
(*Di-more-foe-don*)

Rhamphorhynchus
(*Ram-for-rink-us*)

The last and greatest of the pterosaurs was the North American *Pteranodon*. Its wing span was 25 feet – that of a small airplane! It had no teeth, but a beak like that of a bird. One of the most fascinating things about Pteranodon was the huge bony crest on the back of its head. Some people think that this had to do with the way Pteranodon hunted. Like other pterosaurs, it lived on sea cliffs, and although it occasionally ate insects or small reptiles, its main food was fish.

Using the air currents, Pteranodon would glide low over the ocean surface. On seeing a fish, it would dip its beak into the sea and scoop up the fish. The bony crest added weight to the back of the skull, and prevented Pteranodon's head from being drawn under the water, when it dipped its beak in. Pteranodon had only weak legs, and could probably only scrabble awkwardly about while on the ground.

Pteranodon
(Tair-an-oh-don)

When it got into the air, however, it must have been an impressive sight! Eventually, the pterosaurs all became extinct, replaced by the birds, which could fly better.

The largest land animals that ever lived must surely have been in the group known as the *sauropods*. *Brontosaurus* was 65.3 feet long, while *Diplodocus* measured 90.7 feet from head to tail, almost the length of two railroad cars. Diplodocus could raise its head 30 feet above the ground on its slender neck. It could easily look over the top of a house! This monstrous beast must have weighed almost 50 tons, as much as ten elephants.

Although the creature's legs could support it on dry land, a sauropod usually spent a lot of time wading in marshes and lakes. The water would help its legs to bear its heavy body. In addition, the fierce, meat eating dinosaurs did not like to enter the water, so the sauropod was safer from attack.

Brontosaurus
(*Bron-toh-sawrus*)

Diplodocus
(*Dip-plod-oh-cus*)

Despite their size, sauropods
ate only soft marsh and lake plants.
We think this, because their teeth were weak
and their heads were small. It is thought that they
must have had to spend most of their time eating. The sauropods
spread through most parts of the world, but by a hundred and forty
million years ago, most of them had disappeared, and by seventy
million years ago, they were all extinct.

Stegosaurus
(*Steg-oh-sawrus*)

Stegosaurus was an early plant eating reptile which lived on land. It was slow moving, and its brain was very small, especially for its size: 20 feet in length. It is often said that Stegosaurus had a second brain in its back, above its rear legs. Today, we think that this was a thickening in its nervous system, and not a brain at all.

Antrodemus
(*An-troh-dee-mus*)

Stegosaurus needed protection against the fierce meat eating dinosaurs because it was so slow. It had a double row of bony plates down its back, and huge spikes on its tail. The tail could have been used as a club, when Stegosaurus was attacked. Stegosaurus was one of the first dinosaurs to become extinct.

Antrodemus was a large meat eating dinosaur. It was a two-legged animal, which measured 30 feet from head to tail. However, this dinosaur always walked leaning forward, with its body balanced by a heavy tail. Its back legs were 8.9 feet high: as high as the ceilings of most rooms. The animal's arms were much shorter than its legs, and its hands had four fingers. Its mouth opened so wide that it could have eaten a small reptile whole. Antrodemus probably ate these more often than it ate the larger dinosaurs, such as Stegosaurus.

Many more dinosaurs now began to eat the rich covering of plants on the land. A variety of different plant-eating reptiles developed. Many of them were able to stand on two legs. *Hypsilophodon* was one of the first two-legged plant-eaters. It was quite small for a dinosaur, up to 5.9 feet long – about as tall as a man, although it did not stand completely upright.

Iguanodon was a larger and later two-legged plant-eating dinosaur. This reptile measured 30 feet from head to tail. Probably it had a more upright stance than Hypsilophodon, but it still leaned slightly forwards. Its thumb was a heavy bony spike, which was first thought to be a horn, as we mentioned earlier. Such a thumb would have made a good defensive weapon. We also think that Iguanodons may have roamed the countryside in herds.

Iguanodon
(*Ig-wan-o-don*)

Polacanthus
(*Pol-a-kan-thus*)

As well as small plant eaters, there were also small meat eating dinosaurs. *Ornitholestes* was a meat eater of between 4.9-5.9 feet in length. It stood on two legs, and appears to have been a very nimble animal. This reptile could run quickly, and use its front limbs as hands for catching prey. It probably ate smaller reptiles, amphibians and the earliest birds. Ornitholestes may also have eaten eggs. Ornitholestes itself would have been prey for the larger meat eaters such as Antrodemus.

Polacanthus was a plant eater. It is known from one set of fossil bones, which were found in England, on the Isle of Wight. This was a medium sized dinosaur at 13.9 feet long. It was a four-legged animal, and had a double row of sharp spikes along its back. These helped to guard Polacanthus against attack. There was also a double row of bony plates along its tail. Despite all this armor, Polacanthus seems to have been rather vulnerable to an attack on its side. This probably led to later creatures of a related type having broader, flatter bodies.

Ankylosaurus
(*An-kyle-oh-sawrus*)

We mentioned earlier that Stegosaurus was one of the first dinosaurs to disappear. Its place was taken by other reptiles, such as *Ankylosaurus*. By this we mean that this animal was about the same size, ate the same food and lived in similar surroundings as Stegosaurus. Ankylosaurus, a later relative of Polacanthus, had a very flat body and head. Its body was covered by bony plates and ringed by sharp spikes. In addition, at the end of its tail was a large lump of bone covered with spikes. This tail was a fearsome weapon. Altogether, Ankylosaurus seemed very well protected against attack.

At about this time, there were many crocodiles and alligators in the swamps, lakes and even the sea. Even the first of them looked like the crocodiles and alligators of today. These were called *phytosaurs*, and they had nostrils so far back on their long snouts as to be almost level with their eyes. Later crocodiles and alligators had nostrils at the end of their snouts, just like those of today. Present day crocodiles and alligators have changed little in the last seventy million years.

The last and most successful of the two-legged plant-eating dinosaurs were in the group known as the 'duck-billed' dinosaurs. These reptiles lived in swamps and lakes. They appear to have taken the place of the huge sauropods that we mentioned earlier, which had by then become very rare. The duck-billed dinosaurs were large. *Anatosaurus* measured 40 feet, and *Corythosaurus* was 30 feet long. They are thought to have been good swimmers.

In a few cases, fossil impressions of a duck-billed dinosaur's skin have been found with the bones. From this we have learned that their fingers and toes were webbed. They all had many rows of teeth for crushing soft plants. In order to make room for the teeth, the faces of duck-billed dinosaurs tended to become long, flat and broad, just like a duck's bill! That is how these dinosaurs got their name. Some of these reptiles, such as Corythosaurus, developed bony crests on their heads. We still do not really know what the purpose of these crests was.

Anatosaurus
(*An-at-oh-sawrus*)

There was one more group of plant eating dinosaurs. These were known as the 'horned' dinosaurs. This is perhaps a confusing name, because the earliest of them, *Protoceratops,* had no horn. It did, however, have a 'bump' on its snout which showed where the horn would develop in later animals.

Protoceratops
(*Pro-toh-sair-a-tops*)

We know a lot about Protoceratops, because in Mongolia several of its nests had been fossilized. These contained eggs, young reptiles and adults. It is very seldom that reptile eggs and young are preserved. These eggs were each about 8 inches long.

When adult, Protoceratops was a smallish reptile, 5.9 feet long. It had no teeth, but a horny beak, like that of tortoises and turtles. Protoceratops also had a bony frill around the back of its head. This protected the animal's neck against attack. The remains of Protoceratops have been discovered in many parts of the world.

Unlike Protoceratops, all the later horned dinosaurs had horns. They grew much larger and seem all to have lived in North America. *Styracosaurus* was 14.8 feet long. This horned dinosaur had a frill which was formed into spikes. This gave the animal extra protection against an attack on its neck. Styracosaurus had a single horn on its nose 29 inches long. The whole head measured 6.9 feet and was over 4.9 feet wide.

Styracosaurus
(*Sty-rak-oh-sawrus*)

Reconstruction from the skeleton suggests that, when alive, Styracosaurus weighed about three and a half tons. His name means 'spiny reptile.' Other types of plant-eating dinosaurs relied either on heavy armor, or on running into water for their defense. Horned dinosaurs charged their attackers with their sharp horns.

One of the dinosaurs most likely to have attacked the horned dinosaurs was the terrible *Tyrannosaurus*. This fierce meat eating reptile grew to 40.2 feet in length and stood 20 feet high – taller than a double-decker bus! Its jaw was 3.9 feet long, and contained 6 inch long curved teeth, just like knife blades. Tyrannosaurus was the largest and most feared meat eater that ever lived. However, its hands each had only two fingers and its arms were very short. This dinosaur could not even bring its hands up to its mouth!

Tyrannosaurus
(Ty-ran-oh-sawrus)

Monoclonius
(*Mon-oh-kloh-nee-us*)

Other horned dinosaurs that may have been prey to Tyrannosaurus were *Monoclonius* and *Triceratops*. These too were North American. They were the last dinosaurs to appear. Monoclonius was 19.8 feet long. Like Styracosaurus, it had a single horn. Its frill was not like that of Styracosaurus. It was solid, and without spikes. Triceratops had three horns, a smaller one on its nose and two larger ones on its head. The longer horns were 36.4 inches in length. Triceratops was 30 feet long, and had a reputation as a savage fighter. The horned dinosaurs could probably run quite fast for reptiles. It is thought that like plant eating mammals of today, these reptiles lived in herds.

The dinosaurs had ruled the Earth for over two hundred and twenty million years when a strange thing happened. Within only a few thousand years, the great dinosaurs died out. Almost all at once, the huge flying reptiles, the great sea beasts, the enormous plant eating and flesh eating land animals all became extinct. Only the crocodiles, lizards, snakes, tortoises and turtles remained alive on the Earth. It was as if the reptiles had grown tired of ruling the world, and had resigned in favor of other creatures.

Triceratops
(Try-sair-a-tops)

Why did the dinosaurs die out? We cannot be really certain. It is suggested that the birds, which possessed the ability of true flight, replaced the great winged reptiles, which could only glide. We know that there was a great deal of land movement at this time. The continents themselves began to move across the face of the Earth. Many of the warm, shallow seas were lost as a result. Perhaps the great sea reptiles could no longer survive because of this.

On land, the climate was still getting drier, and a new type of plant gradually appeared. The present day types of trees and flowers began to take over the land from the mosses and ferns. Their stems and leaves were much tougher than those of the ferns and mosses. Perhaps the teeth and stomachs of the huge plant eaters could not cope with the new, tough vegetation, so they died out. When this happened, the huge meat eaters may not have been able to get enough to eat, and they too died out.

There is still much to be discovered about the end of the Age of Reptiles. Perhaps the cause was one of the reasons given above. Perhaps it was all of them. Perhaps it was something yet to be found. Whatever the reason, after the dinosaurs had gone, two groups of animals began to take over. Both were distant relatives of the dinosaurs. On land, there were small furry animals, which bore live young instead of laying eggs. These were the mammals. In the air, there were feathered animals which laid hard-shelled eggs. These were the birds.

The first birds of which we know lived at the time of the great dinosaurs. These were called *Archaeopteryx,* and were about the size of a crow. These creatures looked like today's birds, but there were several differences. Archaeopteryx had feathers, but was unlike birds of the present, whose tails are made up only of feathers. This animal had a tail like a lizard's, and the feathers grew out from this. Another important difference was that Archaeopteryx was a toothed and not a beaked bird. Only the most ancient of the birds had teeth, and there are no toothed birds alive today. Nowadays, all birds have beaks.

Archaeopteryx had claws on its fingers, with which it probably climbed trees. Today's birds hardly have any fingers under their feathers, let alone claws! Archaeopteryx could not have been a very good flyer. Its bones were heavy and solid, unlike the light, hollow bones of present day birds. Its wing muscles were weak. Archaeopteryx probably glided as much as it flew, and traveled only short distances at a time, from one treetop to another.

Hesperornis was a later bird, living at the time of the last dinosaurs. It was a swimming and diving bird, which had lost the ability to fly – rather like the penguins of today. Its wings were very small, its feet were probably webbed, its tail was short, and it still had teeth instead of a beak. Hesperornis was about the size of a goose. It probably swam about on the water surface and dove for fish. Possibly, this was one of the birds that replaced the flying reptiles by eating the fish upon which they depended.

A few million years after the dinosaurs had died out, there were many groups of birds. All of them were beaked and toothless. All had the short, feathered tail of modern birds.

Archaeopteryx
(Ark-ee-op-ter-ix)

One type of bird to appear at this time was the large, flightless land bird. Some of these, like the ostrich and emu, are still alive. Other, still larger ones, have since become extinct. *Diatryma* stood 6.9 feet – taller than a man. It had a huge head with a strong beak. This bird was a meat eater, and a fast runner. It probably ate small mammals, such as the first horses, called *Eohippus*, which were then only the size of a small dog.

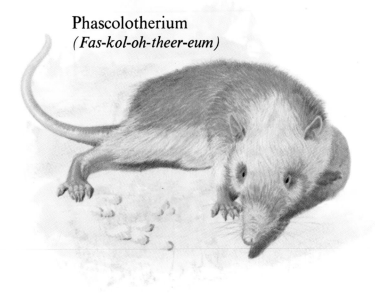

Phascolotherium
(*Fas-kol-oh-theer-eum*)

The earliest mammals lived alongside the dinosaurs. They were small, shrew-like animals, which probably hid whenever the huge dinosaurs passed by. Most of them, like *Phascolotherium,* ate insects or seeds. The mammals were descended from the fin-back reptiles, and reptiles like Dicynodon, but had become very different from them in many ways. They had fur instead of scales, and were warm-blooded instead of cold-blooded. They bore live young, while reptiles laid eggs. The young mammal fed on its mother's milk; the young reptile did not.

These small mammals could develop no further while the dinosaurs ruled the Earth. However, when the dinosaurs died out, the mammals found that they had been given a whole new world to conquer.

Uintatherium
(*Oo-inta-theer-eum*)

50

The scene for several millions of years after the dinosaur extinction must have been rather strange. You see, there were no really large animals alive then at all. The largest were the crocodiles, with a few smaller reptiles, small mammals and some birds. Gradually, mammals became much more numerous, and had a much greater range of sizes.

About thirty million years after the dinosaurs had died out, there were much larger mammals, such as *Uintatherium*. This beast was 11.8 feet long – as big as an elephant. Despite its size, Uintatherium was not a fierce animal. It belonged to a group of primitive, hoofed plant eaters, which are now all extinct.

Eohippus
(Ee-oh-hip-pus)

At around the same time that Uintatherium was alive, a small animal called Eohippus, only 1 foot high, lived on the grassy plains. This animal was the earliest ancestor of our present day horses and zebras. Eohippus needed to run fast, because it was just the right-sized meal for a large meat eater, such as the great flightless bird, Diatryma. Since Eohippus lived on the plains, with nowhere to hide, we can be sure that these animals not only ran fast, but had very keen eyes, ears and nostrils to detect danger, just as horses of today do. Eohippus did not have a single hoof on each foot, like present day horses. It had toed feet, each toe ending in a small, individual hoof.

At this time, the earliest elephant was alive, too. It was called *Moeritherium,* and was only about the size of a pig, but it showed the beginnings of tusks in its upper jaw, and its trunk was beginning to develop. The trunk on Moeritherium was about the size of a tapir's waffly nose. Unlike modern elephants, its ears were small and there were stubby toes visible on its feet.

Synthetoceras was an early plains-dwelling, grazing animal. It was related both to modern deer and to modern giraffes, and was roughly the size of present day deer. This primitive plant eater was peculiar in that it had two sets of horns. One pair grew from the animal's brow, in the way that modern deer horns do. The second set of horns was Y-shaped, and grew from the animal's nose. Sometimes, this front set of horns could be longer than the animal's entire skull! Synthetoceras had to be a fast runner, like Eohippus, to escape the fierce meat eating mammals that roamed the plains.

We mentioned earlier the movement of the continents. This happened, and is still happening, so slowly that if you lived to be a thousand years old, you would not see much change in their positions. However, over millions of years, the continents do drift, some away from each other, some towards each other. If two continents touch, the animals living on one continent mix with those on the other, and they begin to fight for survival. Many types of animals will die out as a result of the mixing.

However, Australia has never come into contact with any other continent. The strange native animals of Australia, called *marsupials,* have been able to survive undisturbed. A marsupial is a mammal that carries its young around in a pouch. The kangaroo is a marsupial. So are the koala, the wombat and many others besides. *Diprotodon,* a huge, rhinoceros-sized marsupial, was a relative of the koala. It was bigger than any marsupial alive today, but is thought to have eaten only fruit and shoots.

Like Australia, South America was cut off from the rest of the world for a long time. Several strange types of animals developed there. These were quite primitive sorts of creatures. Many of them became extinct when more advanced animals came into South America from the North. Others were killed off, much later, by early man.

One of the largest South American mammals was *Megatherium*, at 17.8 feet high. It was one of the ground sloths, huge relatives of those strange animals, the present day sloths, which still hang upside-down in the trees of South America. Megatherium was too heavy to climb trees, but ambled slowly around on the ground. It ate leaves and shoots, and by standing to its full height on its back legs, it could easily reach the upper branches of trees, plucking tender leaves and shoots with its long tongue.

Megatherium
(*Mega-theer-eum*)

Glyptodon was another South American animal. This was a large relative of the armadillo, growing to a length of 8.9 feet. It was completely covered in bony armor, as Ankylosaurus had been, and had a bony club on the tip of its tail. Despite its size, Glyptodon probably ate mainly insects.

Baluchitherium
(*Bal-oo-chi-theer-ium*)

   Baluchitherium was a giant, hornless relative of the present day rhinoceros. At 27 feet in length, it stood three times as tall as a man. However, it ate only leaves and twigs. Its limbs were massive, in order to support its great weight. Baluchitherium ate the leaves from the topmost branches of trees, in the way that giraffes do today. This huge creature lived in Asia about thirty five million years ago.

It is hard to imagine any meat eater attacking this huge beast, but one was able to. The *Sabre-toothed tiger*, or stabbing cat, is thought to have been a most ferocious killer. The animal itself grew to 8.9 feet in length, while its stabbing fangs were 9 inches long. The Sabre-toothed tiger killed its prey in a spectacular way. It jumped on its victim's back, then stabbed it in the neck with its huge fangs, until the prey animal died. A Sabre-toothed tiger feared no enemies. It could kill any other animal. However, after they had existed for many millions of years, it was early man that killed off the Sabre-toothed tiger. Happily for us, the remains have been well preserved in the tar lakes of California. Both prey and pursuer became trapped in these lakes and their bones became fossilized. After all this time, we can still see the marks of injuries and disease on the bones.

Sabre-toothed tiger
(Say-ber-toothed)

For many millions of years after mammals took over the Earth, the climate continued to be favorable to them. Then the Earth rapidly became much cooler. The north wind began to blow much more fiercely, and the trees of warmer climates, such as the oak and birch, were replaced by hardier ones like the spruce, pine and fir. There was snow, sleet and frost. Rivers froze. Many of the earlier types of mammals died out, while others moved towards the equator. Great sheets of ice spread out from the poles, engulfing a huge part of the world. The world was in the grip of the Great Ice Age.

New types of animal, able to resist the cold, began to develop. The woolly rhinoceros, *Coelodonta*, was 7.6 feet long, and had two horns. It had a long, hairy coat to keep it warm. In winter, it would scrape away the snow in order to eat the grass underneath. With a hairy coat, that even had a mane, it is easier to see that the rhinoceros is a relative of the horse.

Coelodonta
(*Seel-oh-don-ta*)

Mammuthus
(Mam-muth-us)

The woolly mammoth, *Mammuthus*, was an elephant with a hairy coat which helped the mammoth to survive the severe cold of the Ice Age in conditions that few other animals could stand. Its huge tusks could be used for shoveling snow off the grass, which it ate.

The warming up of the world, as it came out of the Ice Ages, and hunting by early man, probably made both the woolly mammoth and rhinoceros extinct. However, it is interesting to note that both were alive only a matter of thousands of years ago!

INDEX